Being

Finding your Spiritual Balance

Gently and Sustainably

Aintherese Madden

Copyright © 2025 by Aintherese Madden
Tipperary
Ireland

Paperback ISBN 978-0-9563845-3-9
First Published in 2025

All rights reserved. No part of this publication may be reproduced, stored in a retrieval system, or transmitted, in any form or by any means electronic or mechanical, including photocopying, filming, recording, video recording, photography, or by any information storage and retrieval system, nor shall by way of trade or otherwise be lent, resold or otherwise circulated in any form of binding or cover other than that in which it is published without the prior written permission of the publisher.

The right of the author of her work has been asserted has been asserted by her in accordance with the Copyright, Designs and Patents Act 1988.

The stories in this book are used for demonstration or imaginative expressions. They speak of the author's internal dialogue only and are not a reflection of anyone else's thoughts, opinion or experience.

The author makes no representations or warranties with respect to the accuracy or completeness of this book. This book may not be suitable for your situation. You should consult with a professional where appropriate.

Designed by Callum Jagger

Dedication

To my parents, your legacy of character and faith lives on

To my children, with love

Contents

Preface	ii
Introduction	iv
The Story	6
The Interim Place	11
Populating a Garden	15
Finding the Message	18
Health and Wellbeing	24
Living with Balance	32
Alignment	40
Living in the Moment	46
Prayer	51
Knowledge that Brings Expansion	55
Creativity and Meditation	63
Meditations	65
Connection with a Higher Power	83
Emergence of the Divine Self	97
The Divine Self	107
Recommended Resources	112
Acknowledgements	114

Preface

We are all challenged by similar things in our lives. Using our talents, training to be employable, finding love. Raising a roof, supporting a family. Within that comes the battle of wills, illness, disappointments and grief. Love lost and maybe never found. The excitement of having arrived, success as it has been defined for us, but maybe not by us. The fame façade, disconnection. Our carbon footprint and the shame of time running out. The narrative is one of striving for, moving forward, reaching that goal, and knowing and showing ourselves to the world we live in and experience.

I wrote this book for any person wanting to increase their self-awareness and consciousness. I also wrote it for fellow coaches and health and wellbeing professionals. In the writing of this book, I wanted to be honest, grounded, and sincere. I wanted to write about everyday things that matter a lot, not just to life coaches but to everyone: things we struggle with that make us human, things we find difficult to articulate or things that we don't fully understand, things that cannot be bought or sold, things of beauty and tragic circumstance. I wanted to open the readers' hearts and let them know they are not alone.

I believe it is the ultimate human goal to make

significant connections and not leave this life without reaching out to people and drawing them close. This book is about changing the narrative of your life moment by moment, finding a kindred spirit and a model of fulfilling existence personally and professionally.

Can we afford to compartmentalise our lives any longer? The world is at war but primarily each one of us is at war with ourselves. It is time for lasting change that brings lasting sustainable happiness, peace, and balance.

Come on this beautiful journey with me and open your heart to the possibility of change that really matters. Increase your Spiritual Balance and experience the world from a new perspective, one that is renewable every second of every single day. Choose to look at your life with fresh eyes and become more conscious of the way you think, feel and live. Don't worry about the choices you made in the past. They were the choices you felt were right at the time. Now you can make better choices from a place of grounded self-awareness. A second chance in life. A second chance of living.

Introduction

No matter how hard you try to turn a key in a door; it will never turn if there is a key in the lock on the other side. You can try to knock out the key, break down the door, squeeze through an open window, or call a locksmith. If it happens again, you relive the same scenario. Life is not very different. We have been given a key that fits the lock which turns perfectly to allow us to go where we need to go. Somehow along the way, we lose the key, the key belongs to a different door, we try to use someone else's key, we are shut up, shut out. We may have taken other people's word for it, that this is the door and this is the key.
But we never stopped to ask ourselves:

Why is this so difficult? All I want to do is open the door and go through it.
What is really going on here? Why do I think I cannot do it? Do I really believe that?
Does life need to be this difficult? What can make it easier?
Do I need help? Who can help me?

We do not need to break down the door to get into our own house. We have the right key; we just need to understand how and why this happened and how we can prevent it from happening in the future.

Coaching is a wonderful way of working with the myriad of keys a client brings to the session and helping them recognise the best key for them right now. When I work with clients everything begins with the client's story and where they feel they have been locked out of their own lives. I have included some of my own experiences to guide you on a similar journey of self-discovery. Take this book with you and touch base with it when you feel you need to. Take your time answering the many questions asked. These questions are not just coaching questions; they are soulful questions that open a conversation within you.

Set aside time to practice the meditations, experience stillness and pure quietness. The greater the quality of your experience of silence, the greater your potential as a person. The greater the connection you make with your essential self, the greater your experience of your own Spirituality. Come back to it time and time again until you hear your Calling.

That is my gift to you.

The Story

I grew up on an Irish dairy farm with three brothers and three sisters, my parents and my grandfather, 'The Boss', a man I loved dearly and who has been by my side through it all.

The farm is set against the backdrop of Grange hill. Grange is on the outskirts of a lovely monastic village, in County Tipperary called Lorrha. It was a typical countryside upbringing in the 70s/80s where we helped on the dairy farm after school. We all had our own jobs to do no matter how reluctant we felt. I even remember a time when there were hens, pigs and turkeys as well as cows and cattle. We spent a lot of time outside and as a child, the farm was part of the great escape into a world of imagination. There were nooks, crannies, and holes in the ditches to play. The view from the back of the hill goes for miles and Redwood Castle stands very proud in the distance.

After the steep climb up the hill, there always was a sense of elation and the urge to run and roll down at the other side. For me anyway. There were cowslips in abundance and fresh air that would make your eyes water. My father used to warn me about badgers at the back of the hill that would bite your leg until they heard the bone snap. He said if you had a stick near you, break it in half and you might fool the badger into moving off. That was the only thing that scared me then. I don't think he was serious but then again, I am not sure.

We would lose track of time in the lush green fields and search for adventure instead. It was a gift, and we would reluctantly come home, stopping at every opportunity along the way. I always brought a small bunch of wildflowers for my mother and bathed in her appreciation for those few precious minutes when she woke from an afternoon nap. The hill holds great reverence for me to this day.

We played hurling, went to Mass, and always had a roast on Sundays. The house was small but full of music, dance, debate on the priest's sermon, and a postmortem of the most recent match or any match for that matter. We would stop on the way home from mass for

a block of ice cream from the local shop and urged my father to stop talking lest it melt before we got home. It came with wafers and was a great incentive to eat dinner fast. The girls, including me, were sent some Sundays to the Salesian sisters house at Slevoir, in Terryglass. I can only remember sports days there in the sunshine. When I wasn't on the hill I was cycling, delivering the messenger magazine, and freewheeling down every hill with abandon. It was a time of great freedom and wildness. I felt safe.

The homeplace is so much quieter now and I marvel today at all that was achieved and passed down through the ages; from politeness to politics and everything in between. I have great respect for my parents, who are now unfortunately gone. There were so many of us to care and provide for. They did the best they could during an onerous socio-economic time in Ireland.

Today I find it difficult to manage the needs and activities of two children. That I do alone for the most part, but I do it with great reverence for the miracle that is Birth and the joys that are Children, even if they drive me to distraction from time to time. We have had very hard times and there have been days when I scarcely recognised myself but for the cheeky laughter and jibes that have transformed these babies into teenagers and me into a humbler mother. Amidst a life of constant toing and froing, I find time for Nature, writing, peace, sport and expansion. A Wonder and a Blessing all on the same day.

Taking the time to listen to a client's story, the language they use, the imagery, what they omit, and their breathing all helps create a map of their lives to date and where they want to go. Accurately reflecting to them that story may be the first time they feel heard by anyone. Never underestimate this. That genuine connection can have a huge impact on the client in helping them make a timely breakthrough and reclaim their present-moment wellness.

Isn't it the same for all relationships? If we listened to one another more, we would disagree less.

There is nothing more precious than another human being's story. How much time do you give to listening

to others? What is the quality of your listening? Are you distracted by your own thoughts and needs? What if you were to practice more mindful listening, do you think your connection to the other person would improve? Have you got questions that need to be answered? Don't wait until it's too late to get to know the people you love better. What are some of the changes you want to make in your life that you feel will bring a greater balance of mind, body and spirit? It is fine if you don't have an answer yet. Just reflect on this for a while. This book can help you explore different aspects of your story with the intention of increasing your self-awareness. With increased self-awareness you can recognise areas in your life that have been neglected. Mindsets that have held you back. Emotions that need release. Aspects of your physical body that need attention, nutrition and healing. Revealing your own Spirituality and putting that into daily practice.

The Interim Place

To make a lasting change in one's life one must navigate very turbulent weather and head out onto a road without any certainty. During this time, we can often find ourselves in interim place. The interim place is the space you find yourself in when you have made the clear decision to step away from one part of your life and embark on a new journey. It can come as a shock to people that they are almost paralysed despite their definite intentions for change. Maybe you left the corporate world and are now hoping to start your own business or you have been travelling all your life and now you wish to settle down.

The interim place can come with self-doubt and procrastination. The ego will be very loud in this space because it won't want you to change. It will want you to stay in the 'familiar' even if it isn't in your best interest. This is one of the great times to seek coaching because there needs to be huge awareness around this internal dialogue. Is there any truth in it? Does it serve you any longer? The coach will advocate for you and your dreams. The ego can try to undermine your every move. Without fixing or judging during this time it is important to allow time for direction to come from your inner self, your intuitive self. This requires patience, self-acceptance, and faith. An answer cannot be forced, and a decision made from unacknowledged fear will not be the best decision for you.

Sit quietly for a few minutes every day and just allow yourself to be, despite the discomfort, fear etc. The interim place can also feel very frantic, stressful, scary, and un-grounded, so bring your focus to your breath and allow time to relax. Identify what feelings come up for you around not being able to move forward. Breathe in and out, accepting that the only moment of importance is this one. As any thoughts rush in, or maybe one thought niggles you, just say gently, I hear you, but I am focusing on my breathing right now and I will deal with you later.' Now you are in charge, and the ego must step aside. It will continue to come in, and you will bring your focus back to your breathing. Follow the breath as it enters your nostrils and moves down into your lungs and back out again in the out-breath. This is your time for peace. All is well

.Practicing every day brings this practice into your daily routine. Just keep your feet on the ground, palms turned upwards on your lap in receiving mode and accept with patience that guidance will come. It may be an image, a word, a memory, a person, a statement, or a chance encounter. Take note of your experience each day in a journal/notebook. Thank your intuitive self for guidance and bring your attention back to the room you are in, the chair on which you are sitting. Creative inspiration is coming. This is just the beginning.

Not knowing is knowing.

Continue with this daily practice. It will become a practice you look forward to, and it can be done anywhere. All is well. You are enough. You are loved.

Populating a Garden

Letting go of the feeling of being on the run was a daily task for me after my separation, as sometimes I found myself driving out the motorway not knowing why. In a state of fight/flight. When I felt more grounded, I would stop at the next junction and buy a coffee. Realising the desperate mental and emotional exhaustion, I would get myself home safely and say it would all be ok. I often cried heartbreaking tears for the life we could have had but did not choose. I would breathe in the fresh air and the dappled sunlight. Feeling calmer, my emotions in check, life didn't seem so cruel. And so, I ploughed on. It is hard to explain but if you have experienced extreme fear even just once in your life it hides in the nooks and crannies of your body as a constant reminder that once you felt frightened and powerless. Stress and I were never good bedfellows. The truth is, I didn't want the chaos of the past, but it seemed it was all I knew and constantly tracked me. It was exhausting.

Even when we don't have the answer or the understanding we are looking for, going somewhere we feel more like 'ourselves' is the best start, even just for a moment, because we are saying 'I value myself enough to take time out. I care enough for myself to unlock myself.' The answer you are looking for is not the resolving of Stress, the finding a cure, the revenge, the anger. The answer is not the answer. **There is no answer**. So instead of populating your garden with questions and hoping answers will spring out of the ground, have faith. Harness your creative energies and find the soulful activity that grounds you, moves you towards wholeness, and that you can call upon easily. It does not solve the crisis, but it makes us better able to cope, to never lose hope, and to feel we are in greater control of our world. So, populate your garden with your soul interests and the people you are passionate about. Seek out your wellbeing in the face of adversity. This brings you into the present moment and protects you like a comfort blanket.

You are not your experiences from the past. It does not define your identity today. You are not your fear of what is to come. You are this stillness that you experience right now. The stillness in the resonance you feel as you hear me speak. Between the lines, there is silence and peace. Nobody can take that away from you unless you let them. My mother taught me that. It is like sliding by your greatest fears like a shadow and stepping into your Being. It is breathtaking. Have the courage to begin today.

Finding the Message

My relationship with coffee is very telling as you may have already gathered. When I am stressed, I drink copious amounts of it. I use it to wake up, to fight extreme fatigue, to socialize. To hide out, to feel alive, to build an identity. To be part of something, to have the freedom to choose, to refuse to give up. Sometimes a cup of coffee tastes like dirty ash to me, and I think of cigarettes. But I don't smoke. In fact, I can't stand smoking. Why is this?

When I was a child, my parents smoked thirty a day for as long as I could remember and for as long as they could afford it. It was fashionable at the time and probably a way of managing stress. Anyway, some summer holidays were spent in a smoke-filled car bound for the West, with no seatbelts and only five seats for far too many people or what would be legal in today's terms. We sat on laps all round until the last two mortal enemies sat facing each other in the cubby of a white Volkswagen, knees scrunched up to their chests, trying not to rub off each other. The journey was long and filled with anxious nausea which usually culminated in travel sickness and an embarrassing self-blaming mess.

I dreaded the journey so much. Sometimes I was spared the crowded car when two of us were driven with the local priest and his housekeeper in their station wagon. They meant well. However, those trips were filled with anxiety too, as there was an

Alsatian in the back behind a metal guard. The dog breathed down my neck with his panting and foul breath all the way there. Same trip different day. I would work up the courage to find my voice to say, 'I don't feel well' but by the time the sound would come out, so would the vomit. The car would pull over, the clean-up would begin, this statement would ring true: 'You should have said something,' and the journey would be finished under the silent sticky aroma of repugnance.

Coffee momentarily brings me back to those helpless days and I vow to buy better quality coffee next time or give it up altogether. So, am I addicted to bad coffee or the hold that memory has on me? What does it mean? Am I grateful now for my independence or does it remind me of a time when I felt I had no voice? Do I still have no voice? The adult replaces childhood smoke-filled nausea with a dirty cappuccino and gets behind the wheel of their own car so they can pull over without asking when everything gets too much. It is not the self-coaching formula for health but somewhere in there is freedom, choice, and a great internal mother.

When I am stressed, I drink copious amounts of coffee, maybe to keep my true feelings down. But these same feelings hold me back. Some of these feelings are fear, self-doubt, procrastination. Self-critical voice, paralysis, self-imposed anonymity. Past failure, past hurt, comparison with others.

Thinking not doing, and the 'I am not ready' mantra. The list could go on. I am sure you have your own list. I invite you to be as honest as possible with yourself.

How can we use these parts of ourselves more constructively? One way is to go back and look at our first experiences of these limiting behaviours and beliefs and make sense of it all. Where does the narrative begin and end? What were our first experiences of fear or self-doubt. Can we release these emotions and beliefs to free up our lives? Replace them with positive, life-affirming self-talk. We can change the script. There isn't just one script for your life. You have a choice. You are the author of your own life.

Another way to look at the stumbling blocks along the way is: If something keeps presenting itself then I believe it has a message for you. I also believe that these stumbling blocks don't work in isolation and at the very least have a companion, sometimes an unlikely one. So, what do we have to learn from this?

I found that when I contemplated a new venture, self-doubt would immediately come in. That self-doubt hamstringed me for years. Though I had enough self-awareness to know it no longer served me now that I was an adult., I was still stuck in gear. Why? I realised that there was a duality. Holding onto self-doubt afforded me a lasting connection to family. Without it, I didn't know who I was. Everyone was used to me being largely a silent and diffident person. Also, by approaching things with self-doubt I had already learned to minimize failure and humiliation. So, the reins were always in a state of tension, pulling me back. There was a duality between self-doubt and self-protection. It is fair to say that when self-doubt comes up, putting a healthy self-protective strategy might be helpful e.g. armoring oneself with adequate information or having clear boundaries in place with self and others.

There are endless ways to hold oneself back, to self-sabotage: by being the victim, the rescuer, or the persecutor. By being intensely over-focused, people pleaser, or controller. By not being able to forgive yourself. By not being able to forgive others. I invite you to explore what holds you back and find the message for you in it. The question, "what do I gain by holding onto this belief?' can be very painful as it calls us out on our behaviour. We may feel that we are not the ones that need to change, and we didn't ask for any of it in the first place. However, we may be holding onto these beliefs as a defence mechanism or to get our primary needs met subconsciously.

We cannot move forward until we understand what is going on for us mentally and emotionally. This is essential to your lasting health and wellbeing.

What holds you back and why? Start now and commit to achieving a small change in the next minute, e.g. taking some deep breaths, recognizing a self-critical thought, or stopping procrastinating. Practice mindset shifts ahead of time, rather than during stressful or difficult situations.

Health and Wellbeing

Where and how is health and wellbeing found? It can be in everyday things. Creating a space that absorbs oneself so much that all worries or stresses in that moment dissolve. It could be a yoga class, an old movie, watercolours or a great book. Your thinking expands and gives you the opportunity to look at life from your innate impulse towards wellbeing and abundance rather than lack. If I can do this in one aspect of my life, can I do it in others?

Exercise

Take exercise. Exercise is essential for a healthy body and mind. There is a wealth of support out there to meet the interests of anyone, but motivation and commitment can be low. Unless we find a good reason, e.g., a wedding or a holiday, it can be very hard to start and to make exercise a routine. I find this difficult myself. I always loved to walk but I found I was doing it less. Why? Have I given up on getting into shape or have I just accepted the changes that have occurred in my body cannot be undone? I think it is key to have a level of love and acceptance of your body, no matter what size, age, shape, or season. This is the person that propels you forward, not the person you think
you ought to be. Not the person that is acceptable to others. Inside us all, crowded together are a myriad of traits: fat, feminine, thin, sexy, prude, masculine,

elegant, strong, adventurous and so on. This is your support team. These are your cheerleaders. All of it is ok and makes us well-rounded people.

So next time you decide to take a walk or jog, bring your support team. Don't leave half of yourself at home and apologise for yourself. When we exercise, we feel better and more determined. It is in our best interest to sustain it as a daily practice. So, what is stopping us? Is it that we associate exercise with effort, energy, endurance, and pain? Also, exercising is very repetitive and boring if you cannot assign a greater meaning to it. For me, walking is not just for exercise, it is to feed my soul. If I briskly walk without mindfulness, I come back having done a workout. That's fine. When I walk briskly but mindfully, my posture is better, I am more appreciative, and I feel more positive and connected. My cup is full. How can you assign greater meaning to the task of daily exercise and accept yourself more in the process?

Nutrition

If you have balanced nutrition, you will feel better, have more energy, and look healthier. So why are so many of us unhealthy, struggling with what we put into our bodies and how we maintain them? There is endless information and diet recommendations out there and still, we struggle.

What is it that keeps throwing us back into self-destruction mode?

Our relationship with food is in parallel with our relationship with ourselves. If the self is stressed, then the body is stressed and therefore we don't make grounded decisions about what we reach for. We are managing stress. We grab something that feeds stress, something quick, convenient, satisfying, and self-comforting in the short term. For many, that is coffee. For others, it is something that fuels, like high fat or high sugar. So, we set up a cycle of stress, our blood sugar fluctuates, we get agitated or fatigued and we reach for something again to alleviate the feeling. We know consciously or unconsciously that we are trying to stay going, however we have become suckered into thinking this is the only way. So, we are not digesting what we have eaten or drank, we are digesting the stress and making it more manageable—bite-size pieces, so to speak.

When we are upset, or emotions are running high we can reach for something that will prevent us from experiencing those feelings or reliving pain in part or fully. This may be a pastry or a chocolate brownie. We need mothering and these foods bring comfort even for a short time. It isn't long before we feel guilty about being self-indulgent and giving ourselves a hard time. Or we justify what we are doing by saying we deserve that. I wouldn't have done that if I hadn't been so upset. So quickly you can see a pattern emerging of not dealing with emotions appropriately. There is nothing wrong with

treating oneself. There is a problem when it becomes a coping mechanism.

The same applies to what we drink. Maybe you down fizzy drinks by the litre or lose count of the glasses of wine. Maybe your water intake is so low that you are chronically dehydrated and exhausted. So again, we wash things down, drown our sorrows, and swallow back our tears.

If I look in the mirror, I can see that I have some weight to lose. I can say, 'Well, I have given birth to two children, and I never really got my figure back.' That is true. 'I am constantly driving somewhere.' That is also true but a bit of a generalisation. So, what's the problem here? I am allowing myself to generate too many excuses instead of asking why I don't make a change. The excuses become a wall of armour that layers up and helps me maintain my position so that I cannot lose weight. How much of my weight is diet-related and how much is emotional armouring? The armouring protects me from any criticism from others but does not prevent the ongoing internal battle of feeling bad about myself. The armouring protects me from expressing my emotions.

The lie is not that I think I am healthy when in fact I am overweight. The lie is not that I think I eat a balanced diet when I have an addiction to sugar and caffeine.

The lie is that this is just about food management. It is not. It is about feeding the critic, feeding loneliness, feeding disappointment. Feeding the fear of failure, feeding the fear of true intimacy. Feeding the fear of speaking out and saying no, feeding the fear of embracing my true self.

The lie is saying I don't need nourishment for my mind/body/spirit to feel balanced and healthy.

The lie is knowing this with every fibre of my being and choosing to stay stuck in old patterns of behaviour.

What's in it for me? How do I benefit from this self-betrayal and disconnection?

> Because while it's true, I don't have to change.

While it's true, I don't have to risk discovering who I am without the armouring.

> While it's true, I have that feeling of comfort and mothering.

Everyone is feeding some sort of lie. What is yours?

We have swallowed a message whole about ourselves that is not true. Something someone said or implied, something you read in a magazine or someone you compare yourself with. We cannot digest it. However, the message is so convincing that we believe it. Not only that, but we also work very hard to keep the belief alive. So, we feed it. Why? Well, the why might not be as important because the message may have been passed down through generations or unconsciously become distorted. What is important is: do you believe it?

Mindful Nutrition means we set up a new dialogue and relationship with ourselves. We are not just taking the time to experience and appreciate our food and eat it slowly. We are not asking, "is it too much, too little?" etc. We are setting an intention. We are asking the question 'is this meal in alignment with my goal of greater health and wellbeing?' Is it balanced, nutritious, and tasty? Do I feel good? If I don't feel good, what steps can I take today to get aligned with my daily intention of health and wellbeing? Nutrition is on all levels. We are not just feeding the body, we are nurturing the mind, body, and spirit. That is why diets don't work, because they are addressing an issue on one level only. When you come off the diet, you are quickly back to square one. If we have blocks to good nutrition, then we need to look at where these come from and where the imbalances are. Try to remember a time when you chose something that nourished your soul completely. What did that feel like? Is it something you need to consider again? When was the time you fed your spiritual self with life-sustaining food?

What do you do to explore your spirituality? Are you craving food or just a real connection?

Why do we hold on so tightly to that which is not good for us? Is it that we think that this is all there is to us? If we only look on the outside and disconnect from the inside we lose sight of our essential selves, our voice, our likes and dislikes. A way out of this cycle of poor self-care is to have a mindful approach to nutrition, both food and drink and how we digest our emotions. Creating better balance in our lives.

Living with Balance

Living with balance requires presence from moment to moment, the feedback loop where we can recognize we are off course at the earliest possible moment.

So maybe you drift a little after a negative encounter with family and suddenly recognise that you are out of sorts. This being out of sorts signals that you may have taken on board something that doesn't serve your wellbeing or is not in alignment with your higher values. In fact, that might well be more about their story than yours. So, catching yourself in that moment is vital to facilitate you getting back on track. Adjusting your perception of events is one way that balance can be restored in the mental-body system. However, unless our mental, emotional, physical, and spiritual systems are in balance then wholeness and true balance cannot be achieved or maintained. It takes a lot of work to bring balance to these systems as it requires looking at them in detail, recognising what is out of balance, and identifying actions that need to be taken to restore balance. If one area of your life is very pressurised, then another area needs to be restorative.

Personal perception of the word 'balance' is different for everyone. To be 'out of balance' can be misconstrued as 'off balance'. For some clients, this can be insulting and judgmental. So, when we enter a client's world we are not just working from our definitions, and we need to take time to get to know and respect our client's thought process, experiences, and interpretations—their view of the world. Also, remember a person may have been on such a negative trajectory that they are unable to recall a time of feeling balanced because it is not in their consciousness, e.g., a person who has experienced huge trauma and lived at the edge of their existence for years may find the concept of balance unfamiliar, unsafe, and not a vigilant enough state to anticipate further abuse. I remember loving yoga for years but when I found myself in overwhelming stressful life circumstances, thoughts of yoga frightened me. To relax on a mat, I feared would bring a flood of uncontrollable emotions. I might lose my hold, not only on navigating turbulent waters, but also my hope of maintaining a strong fortification. Something I needed to stay going. Balance is a beautiful state. We need to be certain that we are ready for the process and that this is of true benefit right now. There is no need to rush. We do the work when we are ready to do the work. Here are some areas of your life where you can consider and bring attention to right now.

Self-compassion

Criticism is part of the fabric of society and there is no avoiding it. We have it in the workplace, in newspapers, and on social media. We are constantly criticising each other. However, if we approach everyone with that mindset, then it says more about our lack of compassion for ourselves. Where did this lack of compassion originate? Can you remember the first time that you heard feedback that felt critical? Do you feel it was justified? Our experience of feedback can not only taint how we feel about other's contributions but also hold us back. That fear of potential criticism, what if I mess it up? This can stop us from taking risks. Not taking those risks sets up a dialogue in our heads that further criticises us. We need to identify and let go of those earlier experiences of criticism. We need to question the validity of what was said and look at the impact such beliefs have had on our lives. It does us no good to carry old scripts around with us like they are some sort of security blanket. Nothing is comforting about feeling bad about oneself. It just feels familiar. Nothing is rewarding about annihilating others. What pays dividends is turning down the volume of the bad stuff and turning up the volume of self-compassion.

If you are less than perfect, so what? You didn't succeed but you gave it a good shot-move on. You lost in love-there will be others. If we don't show compassion to ourselves then all our mishaps and failures will be waiting in the shadows to remind us. Compassion makes us more resilient to failure. When you bruise your toe, you don't bang it a second time to soothe it. Learning to be compassionate makes us better with other people, better leaders, and very successful because nothing keeps us down or holds us back for very long.

Self-care

Self-compassion is a form of self-care. Working towards a balanced life of wholeness and wellbeing is another. One thing I see as hugely important is looking at your shadow parts. Those parts of yourself that you are largely unconscious of, the things about yourself and your life that you turn away from, that are hard to bear. They are denied in you for fear they will come out. It doesn't matter how many rituals of self-care you have if something is lurking in your shadow that you feel afraid of, e.g., the victim, rage, shame, greed, abuse, entitlement, sexuality, co-dependency. Maybe your way of working is very manipulative or degrading. Maybe you are a leader with more skeletons in your closet than clothes. We have so many people walking around, many in positions of power, that do not acknowledge their narcissism. Others openly display their self-harm without ever acknowledging they are ruled by their childhood context.

Again, self-care is not care for the parts you like, it's care for the whole self. Working on understanding and integrating these parts paves the way for a greater sense of what wholeness means. The parts we deny deplete our energy. We defend these parts relentlessly or we disguise them. Either way, the shadow part grows.

For caregivers, therapists, coaches, we need to explore why we do this work. Is it your true purpose in life? Are you looking for acknowledgement that you never received growing up? Are you on a crusade? What about co-dependence? What questions are you asking yourself right now?

When you look back over client sessions and the directions they went in, was it more about your needs than the client's? If so, why? Part of the self-care of coaches is asking yourself these questions daily so that you recognise when your own shadow is in the room and negatively impacting the client-coach relationship. Having that greater awareness comes with responsibility, the responsibility to change.

Acceptance of self and others

We cannot change others. Fact. We may want to or need to in our world, but this is one we all must let go. It invites chronic war. Accept that others will never change but accept also that you are human with great empathy. This empathy needs to be channelled towards yourself and those around you. Accept who you are no matter what your experience. Accept others for their story, experience, perspective, and diversity.

Patience to respond and not react

There must be great release in letting it rip. I think if you haven't in your life told someone to 'F' off', then you most certainly held it back. However, as a regular go-to phrase, it speaks more about your reactions to people than your responses. Is what you're feeling in proportion to the perceived misdemeanour? If not, then you are probably reacting rather than responding. You may even be reacting from old constructs.

But does responding make you feel weak and subservient? It doesn't have to. Responding from a place of calm and means what you say will be highly relevant and effective. It will serve your real purpose and be in alignment with your essential self. By reacting you are not presenting the best version of yourself. We all have worked with numbskulls that think that shouting the odds instils respect. But it only serves to make people scared, withdrawn, and fosters avoidance, not contribution, within them.

There is greater personal power in having the ability not just to respond but to choose that response. This may even be just listening. Practice the art of being calm rather than trying to be calm.

Forgiveness

Forgive or don't forgive. Our past is our past. Repeat the past by going over it repeatedly if you wish but you are only causing repeat trauma and microtrauma to yourself. You deserve better than that. Do you want to move on to the next part of your life or are you happy re-living, a chapter of your life, possibly written by someone else. Once you realise that this is what has been happening, then take steps towards forgiving yourself. Forgive yourself because you did not realise the damage you were doing to yourself by holding on to and replaying the detail of the experience. Until you accept this, it's impossible to move on. Looking at people's timeline to date and identifying key moments in their lives can unearth good reasons to forgive themselves. These key moments I have found are never in the height of the trauma or the dialogue surrounding it. These key moments are hidden in the silence in between. We are not just re-writing scripts; we are sifting for gold. This gold represents your core values, your essential self and getting into alignment with it.

Alignment

Alignment brings into clear focus congruence between your values, beliefs, actions and a higher purpose. Alignment is about feeling very connected to oneself and the world around you. This a very relaxed state of Being and is the one thing in your life that you have complete governance over. The jigsaw pieces fit beautifully. You are doing what you were born to do. It becomes your North Star.

Self-Awareness

It's difficult to appreciate the importance of self-awareness until you are faced with a person who has little self-awareness. Being self-aware means, we know our motivations, beliefs, and values. We are not ruled by our unmet childhood needs. We live by our values about which we are very clear. Deepening that awareness brings us into a place of peace, calm, and connection to our higher self. We are in connection with our true purpose, and it is this which brings us back to our centre when we slip into old habits. We are also aware of others, not in a co-dependent way but awareness that is empathic and with boundary.

Comfortable in one's own skin

There is a culture now of celebrities removing their make-up and sharing this on social media feeds. This is courageous but everything is relative to what went before. So, for celebrities, the impact is huge because some look so different. But self-discovery goes deeper than facial recognition. It's making a connection with your true self in the moment. It takes courage to go there and ask for guidance because maybe you have lived a life behind a façade of your own making. This is the body that you got, but you are not just the casing that others see. The more we alter this physical presentation of ourselves the less we will recognise ourselves until we find we are merely a carbon copy of someone else. That person may be beautiful in terms of today's glossy expectations, but wouldn't you prefer to be the best version of yourself? Have that natural glow of wellbeing, intention, and purpose? It is not that you are oblivious to other's opinions, but you care less. You know who you are, where you want to go, the people that you appreciate, and the meaning of your life. You are comfortable in your own skin.

Embodying our true nature

What is anyone's true nature? Only they can answer that. What are your essential qualities? It might be calmness, kindness, adventure. What more can there be? What's in there and behind those eyes? What if there is someone small and fearful or aggressive and scary? What if you are not as appealing to others now? What if this person is a breath of fresh air and just what you need? What if they are honest and authentic? So, we remove ourselves from the external reference and have the courage to present a person who is like no other. To embody your true nature is to wear it inside and out.

Respect

If we recognise the Divine in one another then respect is automatic. Right? But until we have that degree of awareness, it might be nice to make it a presupposition that the people we meet deserve our respect as a minimum.

When you feel genuine respect, you trust people more and therefore allow them more into your world. We are raised with the lesson that 'Respect is earned', but this isn't entirely true. 'On-going respect is earned' because the minute you disrespect a person; they will question your ability to treat them properly in the future. That implies that they began with the position of assumed respect, and you damaged that relationship. Recognising this clear boundary can be very difficult. Particularly if the disrespect is subtle or passed off as jest. The more we let slide by, the more desensitised we become to disrespect. We can explain it away until we blame ourselves. We have now taken on board another person's narrative. Respect has less to do with authority and more to do with value, particularly self-value.

How do you define disrespect in your life? You can bring greater respect to your life based on greater knowledge of what is important and valuable to you. Starting with your wellbeing, what are the non-negotiables in your life? Question assumptions made about you. Question the assumptions you make about others. What assumptions have you made about yourself? What surprises are in store for you, when you do not have to defend yourself against another's disrespect? Who and what have you allowed to trample over you? What do you want to do that is different even if they don't change their behaviours?

Relaxed company

Today we are in contact with people by necessity or design. It may seem like there is no choice. We spend far too much time in the company of people that drain us of our energy, enthusiasm, and resources. Look around you. Whose company do you enjoy and why? Years ago in Ireland, people came together in each other's houses to tell stories, sing, and play music. These same groups of people shared the work of bringing in the harvest and attending mass together at the end of a long week. It was a better time because of the community spirit. Within that is a strong nation that defended its faith, land, language, and culture. These people knew each other well and were at ease with each other. If in the middle of the conversation a cow was calving or stuck in a drain, there were numerous people to call upon for help. They shared their produce and sold their crafts. They celebrated births and waked the dead. I have great respect for them as a proud descendent of an island woman from Scattery. There is a yearning in me for these old ways. Even though, I enjoy the company of people that enrich my life. I go away feeling that I am blessed to know them. Not only do they contribute to my life, but they also challenge it. I feel a sense of expansion in their company. I feel I have been completely myself. But I can count the number of these people today on one hand. I think that progress in this country came at a terrible price. The loss of a good neighbour. What does your choice of company say about you and what would you like to be different? If you could spend an evening with someone new, who would that be and why? Is there someone you haven't spoken with for a while? What does your heart yearn for? Is it more within your reach than you think? What steps would you like to take towards reviving values that are important to you, that are important for the community? There is no time like the present.

Living in the Moment

We have so many teachers of present-moment living. There is great reverence in sharing the experience of it.

The concept that we are not this body, or this mind. Living in the past or looking to the future robs us of this present moment. In this present moment nothing needs to change. All is well. We all practice present moment living and we do not even realise it. Are you aware of an activity that brings you to a place of enormous peace, gratitude, and appreciation? That might be seeing the first snowdrops. But what if we do not have to wait until next Spring to access that beautiful feeling? We can bring our attention and focus into the present moment and visualise Spring and what that means for us using all our senses. This gives us a different perspective on life. We can live from a place of deep connection. The only relevant thing is this perfect moment with complete happiness, peace, and unconditional love.

Love

To be loved is to feel total acceptance without conditions for who you are as a person. It's engulfing, warm, protective, safe, and our basic human right. To feel love can get confusing because we tend to view it from a romantic standpoint or unfortunately just sex. Many of our relationships have the potential to bring love into our lives and create that heart opening that enhances our lives. This may be the people we surround ourselves with, partners, our children, music, art, our accomplishments, or the pets in our care. We all want love, to be loved, to feel love, to feel lovable.

The last one, 'to feel lovable', can be the hardest to convince oneself of. When we do not feel lovable it does not matter who or what is presented before us in the name of Love, we won't fully recognise it, most certainly will reject it, and struggle through life to find or sustain it. It is a very painful existential dilemma. So, if our natural inclination is towards wellbeing, why do we remain unlovable to ourselves? Was a very strong message received somewhere along the line? From whom? Was it true then? Is it true now? Ask yourself: why did you swallow that message whole? Was it love in a twisted, inverted kind of way? What can you do now to detox your mind, body, and soul of this untruth? You did not come into this world to be unloved or feel unloved. You were brought into this world to bring your unique gifts and talents and use them to create your best life and share that with others. You may have had lousy transport for the better part of your life, but let's face it, you need to step out now and start by walking. Walking your own path in the direction you choose. That can be the first act of love for yourself. The second act of love can be to find trusted support to accompany you on this journey. No one should feel unlovable.

Re-Connection with nature

Time in Nature revives the Spirit and blows away the cobwebs. But re-connection with Nature involves that conscious channelling and absorption of the nutrition and energy that comes straight from the ground up through you. It is essential to ensure there is enough fuel in the tank. Your roots run deep and taking time to visualise this positive energy as it travels from the ground up creates great solidity. It reassures us that we are supported. In times of challenge, grounding ourselves in Nature helps to calm our nervous system and create a durability that is unshakable.

Daily practice of meditation and reflection

It can seem impossible to stick to intentions or follow through on tasks unless we have a strong anchor. That anchor may be time, place, practice, or people. You can get up early or designate a place for quiet time. Schedule it on your calendar. Being consistent with one or all of these helps bring reflection and meditation into daily life. Holding to these intentions has a cumulative effect. So, the more

I practice, the greater benefit I receive. The benefit is the certainty of whole-body relaxation, calmness, and clarity of mind. A perfect way to start the day. With clarity comes good decision-making, improved ability to relate to others, but more importantly the flexibility and adaptability that is needed to cope with everyday tasks and the unexpected. I am at my best when I do this instead of dragging fragmented stressed parts of myself around like old boots hoping that at some point in the day they will come together when required. The practice of meditation allows energy to flow freely, connecting us to earth and sky. While energy is flowing freely, we allow healing, rejuvenation, and wellbeing into our lives.

Reflecting upon this feeling of wellness and insight is equally important. The realisation is in the reflection and what you are reflecting is your essential self in the moment. If I am ever in doubt going into a meeting or interview, I merely connect with my daily practice and allow that light to shine from the inside out, that wonderful access to soul-filled light. Our essence comes through in our expression, writing, prayers, music, song, dance, art. It comes from a very ancient place. It is humbling. Explore this wonderful daily practice in terms of your cultural history also.

Prayer

When we pray, we automatically go into a quiet mode. We even go somewhere we won't be disturbed. Silence and privacy to be heard. To be heard by God, the universe or a loved one that has passed away. I remember my father's last task of the day was to kneel at his chair in prayer before he locked up the house for the night. It brought great security to everyone.

I was acutely aware of how deep he was in prayer. With his forehead leaning against his strong hands. He must have left all his worries at the end of the day in the fabric of those prayers with the hope that a solution would come. I sensed that this type of stress could only be caused by money. Being too young to help in adult terms I vowed to be less of an encumbrance.

Despite his own overwhelming stress, he helped others that got into financial or personal difficulty. He didn't judge or persecute; he was loyal and supportive. He didn't hold grudges, and he never asked for anything in return.

I have helped anyone that has come to me with that level of stress because it is the right thing to do. I could never stand by and watch a person struggle knowing that I have three choices, ignore it, compound it or empower the person to find a solution. My father taught me that.

He also taught me the value of prayer and what it

is to be empathic. When we turn to pray our prayers are turned inwards. We pray into the depths of our hearts and souls, awaiting a reply, inspiration, a sign or a positive outcome. We are laying our troubles, those above, below, to our right and our left before someone who has the capacity to hold our story, not shrink away from it and bring us comfort. In my writing I do not promote one Faith over another, but prayer is the one activity that brings us all to our knees and helps us rise again with peace, resilience and connection to our essential self and a Higher Power.

I pray that all people everywhere may realise their own innate beauty, potential, and have the courage to express it in this world.

I pray that you look with your own eyes and find the truth for yourself.

I pray that Love and Respect are both your guides and companions for life.

I pray that ancient wisdom rises in you and frees your soul.

I pray that you find abundance in the everyday things.

I pray that children are safe, loved, and have access to food, shelter and health services everywhere.

I pray that we understand Peace, the kind where no one must win or lose.

I pray that the Love in your heart is shared.

I pray that you experience present-moment peace.

I pray that your story finds healing.

I pray that Nature teaches us resourcefulness and resilience.

I pray that all those we lose in this life are at peace.

I pray our materialism is transformed into appreciation and gratitude for all that is.

I pray that you experience Spiritual awakening and balance.

I pray that you know to pause. If you know to pause, then you know true peace.

I pray that your journey begins today.

Knowledge that Brings Expansion

Commitment to lifelong learning is the way forward. How many brilliant young people slip through the net because they cannot cope with the pressure of an all-encompassing final exam. Or the topics covered bear no relevance to the world in which they live now or want to live. Reading material that fosters expansion is both interesting and motivating. How does this information shape your view of the world going forward? What would you like to do differently. What questions are you asking yourself today, next week? An enquiring and curious mind never stops learning and is emotionally and spiritually intelligent.

Considered thinking

Considered thinking in the moment questions the relevance and validity of what you are about to say but also whether it is necessary at all. It is easy to get caught up in being interesting, better, first with the answer or the question. If we said less, would we have less conflict within and around us? Considered thinking isn't withholding opinions or views, it is considering the bigger picture, the bigger picture being wellbeing. Though I know my opinion or objection, I also know that not reacting is better. So, I sit with the thoughts. I don't feed into my ego by wanting to dominate the conversation. It is ok to let that thought just dissolve and remain quietly engaged with those around me. It is better to listen. This is not the same as having no voice. To the contrary, your voice is loud and clear.

Assigning Meaning

Assigning meaning to our lives reinforces our individuality and unique contributions and helps clarify our reasons for doing the work we do. It also deepens our understanding of ourselves and makes us stand still and view others from a new perspective. Asking a person what achieving this goal truly means for them gives a beautiful invitation for them to access their passion and purpose.

If you cannot 'see the wood for the trees', then finding that greater meaning in what you do opens the possibility of expansion, appreciation, and greater scope of practice.

Challenge

Working with multiple people can be very challenging. Where is the clutter in the room? Who is loud? Who is silent? How do you turn down the noise and turn up the volume at the same time? Knowing yourself and knowing those around you in-depth is essential. It is impossible to align people's values if you don't know what they are to begin with, if you don't know what your own are. Responding with wholeness and wisdom allows you to adapt to challenges and changes the stakes. Why? Because, then no challenge becomes impossible. We don't succeed or fail. We accept that some things need more work or a new perspective. We adjust, reframe, improvise, get real, and look at things from a greater vantage point. What have we learned? What do we need to learn? What are our options, and do we have the energy and resources to meet this challenge? We navigate the difficulties and setbacks with resilience and grace. We are also expanding our Vision. We assign greater meaning to challenge and how we choose to move forward.

Action & Accountability

In every life coaching session, there will be a point in the conversation where action or action steps will be brought up. So, if we only talk about our hopes and dreams, they will remain simply that hopes and dreams. Positive right action steps need to be taken. These are the steps that you come up with. It is you that presents, interprets, and follows through on the actions that help you move closer to where you want to be. However, there must be discipline and acknowledgment that you are now making yourself accountable. Also, you have people around you that will hold you to account, including your family, friends or your coach. Accountability can be a pain because it is great to get so much off your chest during a coaching session. You feel lighter and it does help. You look forward to the next session because you now have somewhere to go with all that is going on in your life. A good coach will hold you to account. Ensure that you clarify your goal, that you take responsibility for your actions or inactions. You don't want to be in coaching indefinitely and deep down you want to champion your challenges. But the hard work needs to be done. If we want health and wellbeing, then we must identify the actions we can take to move towards it. We must follow through each day on our promises to ourselves and we must monitor and measure our progress.

Maintenance and sustainability

Most people fear once they have released their emotional blocks around certain issues that they will slip back into old patterns of thinking and behaving. You will. Every day that you go out, you are like a test pilot. You have no guarantee that your engine won't fail because there are multiple variables that can influence any given day. Lack of sleep, bad news, a health scare, other people, family. So, coaching all areas of your life, not just the goal, is very important. The actions that you want to take have a spin-off effect. They affect you, your family, friends, and work colleagues.

Compartmentalising your goals sets up an outward model of change, that if I see improvement in this one area of my life, then all other areas will follow passively. This is not true, and the singular change you see may start to unravel very quickly, e.g., New Year's resolutions like giving up junk food. What would be a good indicator for you that you are moving closer to achieving your current goals? You might say, well I have increased my running distance or decreased my running time for a run that I do 3 times a week. That is brilliant but how do you feel? Do you have more energy? Do you get up earlier? Have you entered a public run? Has your confidence increased? Does it help manage your stress better? Do you feel less depressed? Are you more productive at work or are you more energetic in your relationships? Has your sex drive increased? Identifying the greater positive impact means you are more likely to sustain the activity.

Coaching for balance in the major areas of your life (health, relationships, finance, career, family, spirituality) makes it easier to work towards wholeness in your life. Looking at what is not working in your life from a more detailed holistic standpoint makes it easier to maintain new habits and sustain a better way of living for ourselves and future generations. We are not just doing the work for ourselves, we are breaking the generational mindset and the inherited limiting beliefs that often we don't understand fully, and we didn't ask for.

Real change

Generally, every good book asks us a question about ourselves or the world in which we live. Is that not the illusion? The thought that we all live in little separate worlds and there is only accountability within that context. When one is resentful and angry, that energy is put out into the immediate surroundings and there is a spin-off effect down the road. The intensity of that energy will determine how far down the road my negative vibe will go. Maybe it's brought in the car with me, to the school gate and back again. Maybe it lies low for a few days and completely overflows three days later. Maybe I snap someone's head off in the shop. Now it's worse because it is out of context, and nobody understands it. So, what I want to do now is get rid of it as fast as possible and try to get back to what I feel is my status quo. Does this seem familiar? This is also true for good vibes. So, what you give out will be attracted back to you. Showing more positivity, kindness, and care comes back to you in the form of appreciation, open hearts, and love. Everything we do affects everything and everyone. We are all connected.

Energetically and though you may not know me, you have arrived upon my book. That is no accident. Why? Because I have been reaching out to you. Right across the world I have been hoping to spread a life-affirming, thought-filled, kind, and spiritual way of living and working. By all accounts I have reached you. Every day I send healing energy to the world because I want to see real change. I want people to value the lives they have been given. I want them to value the lives of others. I don't care what position they find themselves in, even if it is one of great power.

To me we are all energy moving in and around each other, attracting and repelling. But if we stand still and really connect with that flow of energy then we can change things on a global level. If we don't foster an appetite for change, what will our lives look like in 20 or 30 years? There is choice. We all have more personal power than we realise or are utilising. If we approach life with a greater sense of our true value and purpose, appreciation for the here and now, then we make better choices and decisions for our wellbeing, the wellbeing of others, and our Natural world.

Creativity and Meditation

Some people paint or play sport. Others play a musical instrument. It is not something to be forced but greeted like a good friend along the road. You meet and say 'Hello' and by listening carefully it becomes clear what activity or mode of expression to choose. The key thing is that this creative potential is used regularly, daily if possible. Begin mapping out the message you uniquely want to convey to the world. If we keep our creative talent hidden or to ourselves then we miss an opportunity to light up someone else's world.

This has helped me craft the life coach I am. For me it is a great gift to know where my creativity can take me but also to help others along the way. Finding ways to harness my intuition and creative thinking has been key to deepening my understanding of life. In this space I have the freedom to express my deepest thoughts and translate them into beautiful meditations, prayers, poems, journal entries, and of course this book. I have shared some of my meditations below that I have found to be profound and healing. The natural flow and sequence of these meditations are offered to help you to connect with your essential self and a higher power. The meditations can be done in sequence over time or individual meditations can be used in isolation. Go with your own gut feeling and intuition.

Meditations

At this point we must consider how we might practice emotional and spiritual wellbeing. Meditation or any quiet practice may not come easily to you, particularly if you run or lift weights to de-stress or think it's a whole lot of nonsense. It takes practice, dedication and self-discipline. But most of all it takes a leap of faith and surrender. So, if you are new to meditation or re-introducing it into your life, it is worthwhile to set up a space where you will not be disturbed for at least 10 mins initially. Maybe early morning before everyone starts their day. Some people like to create a small altar space with some flowers or a candle or an artefact of meaning to them personally. If you don't want to meditate, then substitute the word, possibly prayer, reflection, quiet time, grounding, self-connection. Whatever puts you in a comfortable non-judgmental place.

The time meditating can be increased slowly until you can tolerate sitting for longer periods of time. But begin by using this time to sit comfortably supporting your back, feet flat on the ground, and just observe your normal breath as it goes in and out. The oxygen passes through your nostrils and down through your airway, into the lungs. CO_2 is then exhaled, and the cycle begins again. Consider how amazing the human body really is. We don't tell the lungs to breathe or the heart to beat, they do it automatically in support of living. We notice the feeling of calm. Our heads are clearer, and we may wonder why we didn't do this exercise sooner. The relevant part is that we are now doing it. Any other self-critical thought is just noise, it comes, it goes, it is gone—but we are still breathing.

What intention would you like to set for the day? An intention might be to be more helpful or friendly to co-workers, to drink more water, to use only positive self-talk. Place a reminder where you can see it and if you find yourself slipping into old habits just return to your breath. In your own time, build your experience with meditation.

As your practice deepens so does your experience of silence and the richness of the silence between words. Within this silence is the pure potential of all beings. Practice a particular meditation daily until you start to feel the benefits. Try some of mine below. Write about your experience in your journal. Write about the feelings, sensations, images, memories or words that come up, in order to process them. What thoughts did you have later, or did you notice anything new? Reflect on what you have learned.

Lavender Meditation

This lavender meditation below is a lovely meditation and will really enhance your life. It is very calming. It also reminds you just how powerful your senses and internal memory are. If you would prefer the scent of another herb or flower, then please choose that.

- Take a bunch of fresh lavender or a scented flower you love and hold it in your hands. Observe everything about it.
- Sit comfortably with your feet flat on the ground and your eyes closed softly.
- Gently hold the bunch of lavender.
- Breathe in for a count of four and out for a count of five.
- Repeat three times.
- Now, gently raise the lavender to your face and breathe in this natural scent.
- Allow the scent to slowly float over you and through you.
- Observe yourself coming to a relaxed calm state.
- Breathe normally without force.
- Practice visualising the lavender: the form, the color, the texture, the scent.

- Repeat the exercise again.
- Repeat for a few days, two or three in succession. You are practicing bringing the scent to memory.
- On the 4th day, repeat the meditation without the lavender.
- Repeat the steps, imagining you are holding a bunch of lavender.
- Call from memory the form, colour, texture, and finally the scent of the lavender. Yes, you will be able to smell the lavender.
- You have learned to internalise the scent. It is a great skill. You know that this scent is relaxing and calming. You can call upon this skill anytime, anywhere you need to feel a sense of calm and ease.

Positive switch meditation

When you may be feeling at your worst or you have argued with a particular person again, your head can be full of chatter. Maybe you've had a bad day at work, and you feel self-critical or very ungrounded. Maybe when you look in the mirror you do so only with judgment.

For this meditation, bring all those mixed-up feelings and negative thoughts and just sit with the discomfort, the noise, the stress.

- Begin by taking a few normal breaths followed by some deep breaths.
- When you are ready, slowly breathe in for a count of four, hold for a count of four, and breathe out slowly for a count of five.
- Do this slowly and gently for a couple of rounds of breathing.
- Take your time and respect your own limitations.
- This will bring you into a very relaxed and grounded space.
- As your thoughts wander in, just breathe normally.
- Catch your mind in the act of trying to feed you a negative thought.

- At first, there will be resistance—return to your breathing and continue.
- Acknowledge that this negative thought no longer serves you.
- **Do I believe this anymore?**
- **Was this ever true about me?**
- **Where is the evidence to prove it?**

Each time negative self-belief comes up, you have the courage to ask yourself the questions above and then replace it with a more life-affirming one. A belief you know to be true about you now, and you have evidence to prove it.e.g., *I am a failure*

I did not succeed this time, but I have learned how to approach things differently.

e.g., *I am no good*

There are some things I need more help with but in general I am very good at my work.

This process of challenging negative thinking and self-limiting beliefs can bring up huge emotions as you slowly realise how you have been ruled and conditioned by others. This work is done slowly and methodically with a lot of process journaling. Make this a daily ritual to catch yourself in the act of negative thinking and immediately task yourself with switching to a more positive mindset. You have been conditioned to believe these things for a very long time. These thoughts won't magically turn off. The positive switch meditation can be practiced daily, but the switch can also be made in the moment from negative thinking to more life-affirming thoughts. This will become a particularly good habit, and you will even become very aware not only of your own compulsive negative thoughts but also of others'.

Following on with cleansing meditation will remove the toxic effect of negative thoughts, some of which you may have swallowed whole. Don't be hard on yourself and keep up the good work with the self-loving kindness meditation also.

Cleansing Meditation

This cleansing meditation takes time. So, allow yourself at least half an hour to devote yourself to this practice. It can be used as preparation for going into or coming out of difficult situations. It cleanses the energy, centers you, and brings you back to equilibrium. Why might we need cleansing meditation? There are people in our lives that we cannot change but we must still navigate. Having tools that keep us grounded and connected to ourselves prevents us from losing ourselves in the company of these people or in the face of adversity. Emotions can be very close to the surface as we consider this. This is not unusual because when the body comes to rest it may not have had that opportunity for an awfully long time. I know, many people may not fully understand what you are going through or struggling with. Hang in there. You are doing this for yourself, no one else.

- Take a moment to sit comfortably in a space where you will not be disturbed.
- Put your feet flat on the ground and close your eyes, palms gently laid on your lap.
- Breathe normally.
- Sit with your emotions, allow them to be what they are without analysing.
- Breathe, in a relaxed unforced way.

- Breathing will become much deeper once your chest has relaxed.

- Allow the feelings of agitation and unsettlement to just be there also.

- When you find yourself going up into your head, gently come back to your breathing.

- As you feel that beautiful sense of peace, allow it to flow to each part of your body. You are not trying to change anyone or change yourself; you are seizing a moment, a break from it all, and shifting your focus. When you are centered you are stronger and much more resilient.

- Now gently bring your breathing to your eye area and behind your eyes.

- Quieten down the voice in your head.

- In a moment you will notice some shimmering behind your eyes like shimmering sunlight on the sea. It may be as small as a flicker.

- Build on this image and visualise this shimmering light starting to fall like glitter in water.

- The falling glitter gently moves throughout your body from your head all the way through to your feet into the ground, cleansing as it goes. Removing toxins.

- You can gently feel it pass through each organ, along your arms, hands, legs, feet.
- As it moves it leaves behind a shining light that lightens the mood and brings positivity and hope. Bask in this light. Breathe it in.
- Wait until the glitter has completely settled and the body is at rest.
- Bring your attention back to your breathing, the chair you are sitting on, and the room. Open your eyes.
- Bring your hands together in prayer pose and bow your head.
- Give thanks for your ability to self-care, cleanse, self-heal, and self-protect.

Note: This is a very effective meditation, but I would suggest doing the following while you are mastering the technique or if you need help at any given moment. Fill a recycled jar with water, maybe 3/4 full. Add a generous amount of glitter, including gold. Put the lid on and shake the contents of the jar. Hold the jar in front of you. I sometimes have a salt lamp on in the background. Watch the beautiful glistening glitter settle. **Breathe**. Totally focus on the glitter. Breathe in gently and breathe out gently. That will trigger a similar process consciously or subconsciously in your body of settling, relaxing, letting go, coming to rest, cleansing, and finding your centre and sense of peace again. Try it.

Self-Loving Kindness Meditation

A suitable time to do this meditation is when you feel a sense of failure or self-criticism, or you want to follow on from the positive switch or cleansing meditation.

- Sit quietly, and though your mind may be very busy just sit with these thoughts.
- Breathe gently as you have already learned.
- As the impact of a sense of self failure is very immediate, create greater space between you and your inner critic by saying to it:
- Quiet down now. I hear you but this is my time now. I will deal with you later.
- Start to notice these critical thoughts lose their power and fade a little into the distance.
- They won't go completely away, but they won't remain in the foreground.
- Now place one hand on top of your other hand gently in an act of self-care and say:
- *I am more than my thoughts*
- *I am more than my problems*
- *I am more than the labels*
- *I am loved*

- Repeat until you feel that sense of connection to yourself.
- As you feel self-connection, breathe and allow the positive feeling to permeate your whole body. Repeat:
- *I am accepted*
- *I am forgiven*
- *I am learning*
- *I am loved*
- Breathe in this moment of peace, self-acceptance, self-forgiveness, and increased self-awareness.
- Return to the room when you are ready.
- Ground yourself by making connection with your feet on the floor, the chair you sit in, and your surroundings.
- Journal your thoughts later.

Loving kindness of others

To spread loving kindness, e.g., random acts of kindness not only improve the lives of others, but they also enhance your life too. We've all experienced the surprise casserole on the doorstep, the coffee that was paid for anonymously, a card that was beautifully procured. Some people are better at giving to others. By the same argument some people are better at receiving kind gestures. Somewhere there can be a feeling of not deserving good things. That fills me with great sadness because every human being is worthy of kindness, big and small. Unfortunately, daily kindness isn't everyone's experience. We cannot change the circumstances of another person's life, but we can help to improve it.

This loving-kindness meditation helps spread loving kindness to the people you meet every day: your family, colleagues, friends, community, people around the globe, etc. You can visualise a specific person or wait to see who appears before you:

- Practice in a quiet peaceful place.

- Speak in a clear way, saying <u>one</u> of the phrases below or one you deem more appropriate will come to you.

- *I see your uniqueness*

- *I see God in you*

- *I see you*
- *I wish you well*
- *I wish you happiness*
- *I wish you health*
- *I wish you strength*
- *I wish you abundance*
- *I send you love*
- *I forgive you*
- Give this gift without expectation of anything in return.
- Let go of any desired outcome.
- Open your heart as you visualise yourself sitting in the presence of this person. (In that moment you might be surprised at who stands before you in your visualisation. Go with the flow).
- Give with love, peace, kindness, and forgiveness if that is ok with you.
- Breathe and stay connected to yourself and the other person.
- Give thanks.
- When you are ready, let them go on their way.

- Practice this exercise often and you will find when you meet that person or other people in person you will have a greater appreciation of them as they are, without ever saying one word.

Meditate for Pause

Bringing 'a pause' into our daily routine is essential. Learning to disconnect from agendas, pressure, and outcomes relieves stress, brings us into the present moment quickly, and reminds us to slow down. Right now, I need to take a moment. I know I have a deadline or a meeting coming up, but this moment is for me, my health and wellbeing, and believe it or not the wellbeing of my family and colleagues. In this moment I just breathe, the past is gone, and the future is not yet here. This is a perfect moment. It is in the present and in this silence that I am at peace. I am well.

Practicing meditating for pause is helpful in disconnecting and letting go of outcomes. Wellness and peace are here right now at this moment. There is no failure. There is no outcome. There is just absolute peace. Letting go of the outcome is not letting go of the desire to achieve your goal. You are letting go of the critical inner voice, fear of failure, worst case scenario, finite mindset, comfort zone, self-doubt, limiting beliefs, grasping and disempowerment. Introducing these pauses throughout your day will clear your mind, ground your body, and nourish your soul.

- Just stop completely what you are doing and just be in the moment.
- You will not get a moment like this again.

- Stop rushing, racing, keeping up, passing out.

- Pause.

- Let everything just pass by you for a moment.

- Now, oxygenate this state of mind by taking a deep breath.

- Hold that breath for five: 1, 2, 3, 4, 5.

- Exhale, being mindful to bring that exhale right down through your base chakra to the ground.

- You may feel tingling in your feet as the energy passes through them.

- Wellness in this moment, is letting everything go.

- Continue to breathe deeply for three to four breaths and then let your breathing come back to normal.

- Bow to this part of you that knows the wisdom of a 'Pause.' Let go of the struggle and swap it for peace, ease, grace, self-assurance, trust, faith, and self-belief. You are now in receiving mode. You are receiving a great gift. It doesn't get much better than this. *Right now, this moment is You. You are in it and of it.*

Connection with a Higher Power

Soul-searching

If we know that we are energy beings housed by the human body,
then what is the soul? My belief is that the soul is the connection we have to that energy. So, when we are going about our daily lives we need to tune into those moments when we feel appreciation, gratitude, pain, love, joy, and happiness. We are deeply connected to our soul. When we walk in the forest, the soul resides not just in the trees but in the stillness, sounds, sense, the dappled light between the trees, and our sense of it all. When we walk on the beach, the soul shows up in the breeze, shells, crashing waves, and in our unwillingness to leave. There is always a pull to stay longer, so stay longer. Soul shows up when you receive a hug. When that hug is lost, even forever, the soul shows up looking for connection to a warm blanket, open fire, trusted friend, or a beloved pet. The soul is always searching for that connection. You must show up as this person connected to your own energy and be aware of what you need to make that connection. Where is your favorite place to go to? Where do you like to walk or run? What creative activities do you love to do or have always wanted to do? If you were to reach out to a person right now, who would that be? In coaching we witness

the soul in our clients as we see their eyes light up or their breathing relaxes and expands. Sometimes the client is not aware that they have lit up and reflecting that back to the client can bring positive self-awareness and connection in the moment. That is how close you are to your essential self, your soul self.

Wisdom

Some of us feel real connection to our ancestors because we grew up with them in our homes. However, others equally find connection through historical figures, mentors, books, travel, and nature. When you feel that connection, it is amazing. You feel supported, grounded, stronger, and have a real sense of belonging. Suddenly there is an awareness of your tribe, the place you came from. No matter which way you make the connection, it is very real and wonderful knowing that it can be tapped into as needed.

During a weekend group training many years ago I participated in a 'Family systems' workshop. In family systems therapy, one of the things a client looks at is the literal order of their family and where their actual place is in it. This includes births, deaths, and miscarriages. It can be hugely beneficial when a person feels a certain disconnect or a sense of not belonging. It is also hugely powerful at dealing with loss and grief. Clients place their family using people from the group, naming who will be father, mother, siblings etc. Essentially setting a stage. They allow space for anyone that has passed away or any miscarriages. Immediately you feel this deep connection with the dynamics of their family, and it is a truly powerful way of working.

For some clients they must go back several generations to find a supportive relative. During the workshop one student lined up the other female participants in a generational way, one behind the other. They spent time connecting with each woman. Their intention was to find a woman supportive of women. They had to go back five generations. When this person looked out at them, they seemed to know immediately who they were. We could feel their gratitude that there was someone there to support them. We could also see the generations of women that were unsupported. It was heartbreaking to watch.

We can latch onto our past experiences and feel that nothing will change. The power and support of ancestors is vital, particularly in a world where we may no longer live with grandparents and our lives are moving at such a fast pace. Use the visualisation to follow and gift yourself support from your ancestors. These people are not only your family. They are also your wise friends.

The Visualisation

- Visualise yourself taking a walk along a wild unspoiled beach at a time when you have it all to yourself.

- You are wrapped up warm and in no hurry.

- Keep going until you come to a stoney area set back from the shore.

- Walk along the big stones carefully until you can hear them knocking off each other.

- Be mindful of how old these rocks are and how much life they have experienced.

- So, walk with care. They are all different.

- Connect with the sound of the stones as they clack and rock under your feet.

- You can hear the sea crashing in the background.

- The wind whips across your face, dragging your hair every which way.

- At some point you will get a sense of ancientness and soul connection that feels unique to you. It may come from the direction you feel drawn to.

- Remain open to the connection.

- Keep going with mindful and reverent steps.

- Each step brings you back to a distant time.
- You begin to feel a part of something great.
- A sense of belonging and a sense of something greater than yourself.
- When you find a comfortable rock, sit facing out to the sea breezeNow visualize a wise ancestor, guardian Angel, or a mentor coming to support and comfort you.
- Take time to visualise this wise ancestor in detail as it will make it easier to call upon them later.
- What do you see? Were they holding anything? Where were they standing? Did they call you along a path? Were they far away and you had to walk towards them?
- Do you have a sense of who it is? It doesn't matter if you don't recognize their actual face. They may not be facing you or they might be surrounded by light.
- Listen carefully.
- They may have a message or a gift for you.
- Listen for any words of wisdom.
- Do you have a question to ask them?
- Take all the positive energy and support that is freely available to you.

- Express your gratitude and vow to return.
- Leave carefully in the knowledge this could be a ritual for you.
- Give thanks for this very deep connection to yourself. Slowly bring your attention back to the room you are in, the chair you sit on.
- Move your feet and hands and begin to open your eyes.
- Carry this positive connection with yourself throughout your day.
- If you lose connection momentarily, place one hand on top of the other and just repeat, I am loved and I am not alone.
- Take a deep breath and relax.
- You are never alone. Journal about your experiences and each time bring clear intention with you.

This experience takes in all senses, but it also is such an energetic connection. Practice visualisation regularly or physically travel to your favourite wild beach location. I found the more often I walked on actual rocks the more solid I felt, the more sense my life made. Two places I love to do this are Kinvara beach and White Strand. I am sure you have a spot close to you too. If you do not have a sense of who it is you are connecting with, you may find that your tribe is not related to you in the traditional sense as I said earlier. Be open to this as it will open a whole new world for you.

Heart Rejuvenator

You can use this meditation to focus on your heart and heart space. Your heart may be broken, weary, ill, grieving, or searching. Alternatively, you can focus on other parts of your body. If you can do this meditation outside, it is even better.

- Sit in a comfortable chair or bench with your feet flat on the ground.
- Feel the support of the chair.
- Give thanks for this time you have set aside for yourself.
- Let's stop, breathe gently, and fully let go of the day you just had.
- This is your space, your time to rejuvenate.
- Close your eyes.
- Bring your awareness to your body and feel the air coming through your nose travel through to every part of your body.
- Notice any areas of the body that are tired, sore, uncomfortable, or feel strange.
- Notice the parts that feel good.
- All are welcome.
- Breathe gently into your heart space.

- Your heart becomes calm and relaxed as you nourish it.
- Visualize a white light filling up your heart.
- Connect with this white light which is pure positive energy.
- Observe as it radiates to every part of your body and you light up inside, in the same way as you might light up when you receive a compliment or fall in love or feel joy.
- You can now create this positive energy yourself.
- Consider how far you can extend this light. Each time you do the meditation you will notice the light is brighter and extending further.
- You are connecting your energy to the world around you. The world around you is connecting with you.
- Bring your focus to your feet and notice the light change to a multicolored light.
- It is coming up through the earth, through your feet and up through your body.
- This energy of beautiful colours fills your heart and rejuvenates it.
- This light represents love.
- You are bathing your heart in a sea of vast

potential.

- When you feel you have enough, give thanks for this nourishing energy and then let go with ease.
- Bring your awareness back to your body, your feet on the ground, your hands in your lap, the seat on which you are sitting.
- Slowly open your eyes and adjust to your surroundings knowing that you can return to this beautiful pure consciousness again whenever you need to.
- Don't hold on so tightly.

Breeze meditation

When I first experienced this connection, I was sitting in the window of our former home, feeling very broken and alone as I knew our house had to be sold. Then something caught my eye. It helped me awaken that deep connection to Nature that I once had. Gently it became easier to let go.

- This meditation is done sitting at a window or in a park. If you are short-sighted, you will need your glasses.

- Sit in a comfortable position and put your feet flat on the ground, place your hands gently in your lap.

- Softly allow your breathing to rest.

- Breathe gently without force.

- Close your eyes and breathe in for a count of four and out for a count of five.

- Repeat three or four times until you feel calm, relaxed, grounded, and the chatter in your head has quietened down.

- Open your eyes and gaze upon the first thing you see—this may be a houseplant or an ornament.

- Take in its shape, form, and colour.

- Cast your gaze out a little further to

flowers, shrubs, hedging outside.

- Take in its shape, form, and color.
- Can you see the breeze catch the leaves?
- Observe the gentle sway.
- Breathe gently as you allow yourself to connect with this energy.
- Cast your gaze a little further to the trees in the distance.
- Can you see movement? Look carefully.
- Rest your eyes in the sway and allow it to soothe your heart.
- This is the healing power of Presence.
- Come back to the houseplant and again look to the flowers, the shrubs, and then beyond to the trees.
- Now you are making connections more readily.
- Do you sense the connection between all things? The connection between your breathing and the movement of all plant life.
- Are there birds? Are there clouds moving?
- Are there light shadows?
- Breathe in your universal connection to all living things and allow this connection to

heal you.

- You are truly connected and loved in all that you do and all that you are.
- You are holding Presence

Emergence of the Divine Self

Moving from surviving to thriving

What prevented me from making better choices and committing to those choices? All I knew was survival. Survival maintains you in a constant state of vigilance, stress, anticipation, fear, and anxiety, always on the ready. To step across that bridge felt like my whole world would become insecure. It felt unsafe. I felt that I would get intercepted on the road and made turn back. Was it unsafe or just unfamiliar territory? Surely, I didn't want to keep my old life. When I cross over, what do I do? Who am I? Would we survive?

I wanted something more for us. We needed better. We deserved better. I needed to let go of fear to do that. If I didn't, I would have to keep my old life forever which frightened me more. My reason became wanting to do more than just survive. I wanted us to thrive. Now I work on sustaining that thriving to have that stronger, deeper connection with a higher part of myself. I want to experience the love and joy I have for myself, my family, and the world around me without limitations. I want to share that with others. To thrive is to live with reverence, appreciation for myself, the people I live and work with, and every living thing. To thrive is to breathe freely.

How do we encourage the true, congruent, and divine self to shine through?

Giving thanks

A daily gratitude journal allows you to set the tone for the day. Start by writing these simple words, filling in the blanks for yourself:

I am grateful for………. because……….

For example: I am grateful for my family because I experience that deep connection which I value so much. I am grateful for all the abundance around me, the trees, the birds, flowers, the changing seasons, friends, family, and the water I drink, the food I eat, the home that shelters me. Make it a daily practice to write in your journal at least 3 things that you are grateful for. When you read back over your journal there will be evidence of all the positive things in your life. We forget easily but not for long. Contributing to your journal means that a day doesn't go by that you haven't felt appreciation. A life of gratitude brings abundance. The greater the appreciation, the greater the abundance.

What are you most grateful for today?

Where in your life can you show more gratitude?

When life is going wrong, and everything seems to be conspiring against you, it is difficult to feel gratitude. I know this from my own experience of having to move house several times. I missed terribly what I had lost, and I was anxious for what the future held. I didn't feel grateful. I felt robbed, unreasonably challenged, and completely at the mercy of other people's decisions for us. My health was suffering. Then I happened to be lighting a candle in a church one day and there was a novena prayer which culminated in the words 'help me not lose heart.' It didn't say 'help me have hope"; it was don't lose heart. Hope felt like something in the future, and I was asking for help right now. In that moment I realised that if I didn't lose heart, I wouldn't give up. I had the strength to keep going, and it energised me. So, I am also grateful for those serendipitous moments that remind me that I am not alone, and that you are not alone and that we all are being guided in the gentlest of ways. It is pure joy.

Relishing Joy

Joy for many people is a welling up of happy feelings almost overflowing. It is a perfect state of happiness. All is well in that moment. Our emotions, mindset, physical habits, actions and inactions influence our energy vibration. Joy has a high energy vibration and when we are in this state, we can draw many positive things to us—positive emotions, love, abundance, and health.

To recreate that feeling, practice sitting quietly and recall the events that created that feeling of joy for you in the past. Which senses were involved? What do you see, feel, hear etc.? What colours surround you? Are you a specific age or is it set in a much-loved location? Breathe into this space knowing this beautiful state has been created by you. Absorb that light and energy and allow it to soak through your whole body. Notice that it is greater than your body or mind. It comes to you through a memory, a photo, a scent, any kind of deep connection. You are creating joy in your life.

It is out of silence that this pure joy will come. It is ethereal. It is you.

Listen for your Calling

When I was young, I had some sort of a 'Calling'. I used to read a small bible, pray, cycle to the church regularly, and roam the fields feeling I was part of it all and spiritually free. I knew to go to the trees. I would sit under them and there was comfort, peace, and hope in that moment. I could hear the leaves rustle. I could feel the wind swirl all around me. There was nothing between me and nature except the instinct to come and sit there. I never felt embarrassed by such knowings. I never needed convincing. As a child, sitting under the tree comforted me like no parent could. My tears would go away, and I felt balanced and grounded again. I felt it in my breathing. I could hear the rustling leaves in my ears long after I got home. It calmed me. I was silent in a good way. Is that all that separates us from peace, love, freedom, connection, belonging? Hearing the instinct to go and acting on it? Did I know how enormous this was at the time? No. Did anyone else know? No.

As conditioning became stronger than my natural impulses and intuition, I lost touch with this part of myself. This was a huge loss to me, though I didn't know it at the time. I travelled through life looking for something that was missing. How could I bring this into being when I didn't know what it was or where it came from? I started asking myself deep questions: Who instructs me? Who have I let instruct me in the past? Who does Nature take it's instruction from?
Things started to catch my eye, like a branch moving or light streaming through the hedge, and I would stop, look, and feel. There it is again, that reminder of the Universal connection between all things, Beings, me. I could see the abundance of life as the seasons changed, as birds came, rested, nested, and went. As fruit was formed, eaten, and renewed. Life was everywhere around me. I acknowledged it. My attention would turn to my lungs and heart. I could feel my heart inside my chest. My cells being nourished. Toxins being removed. The constantly

revolving circle of life that does not destroy hopes and dreams, shatter confidence, or condemn one to misery. The connection is light and full of nutrition. And breathing into that abundance, I realised I was blessed to know my own Being.

I can connect with this energy anytime. When I find myself off course it is easy to steer back to the present moment because it is the only moment that we are truly living. Right now. The present is where you are at your best because you have let go of attachment to outcomes, forgiven past failures, and trust that the future will take as good care of itself as this moment and each moment after it. As I breathe in, it is already in the past. As I breathe out, I know I will automatically breathe in again. I have no doubt. Right now, I trust in nothing other than my own knowing. I have Faith. I know the more I practice this wondrous connection with all of life I am more content, loving, patient, and at peace with anything that happens around me and within me. In that space I can forgive anything because my gratitude at this unexplained abundance is far more important. My reliance on this connection helps me face any kind of adversity, to celebrate life, and to connect with Nature and that Higher Power.

Discover your life purpose

I participated in numerous peer coaching sessions during my life coach training, to practice my skills. During one of these coaching exchanges, I had an amazing experience. I contracted to work with a fellow coach for six sessions even though I felt uncertain at the time whether we were the best fit for each other. I was there to learn. We clashed from the get-go. I dreaded the sessions. The hour was structured with lengthy biographical questionnaires that clearly were coach centred and leading. I could not wait to be finished and move on.

It is no surprise that I quickly went into a transference relationship with her. Transference is the unconscious redirection of feelings and attitudes about a person in the past onto a person in the present. Coaches don't cross over into Psychotherapy but someday, one of your clients or even family may go into a transference relationship as I did. It is up to you at that point to run for the hills or ride out the storm. I think one of my sentences began with 'I don't give a f**k.' The coach pivoted in the moment, recognising my potentially explosive misplaced anger but also from previous sessions my propensity for the visual. She manoeuvred me to connect. This probably wasn't the best move on her part as that could well have fuelled my anger. I had enough self-awareness at the time to go with the flow. She knew my anger was not out of control. So, I was invited to connect with that part of myself. Which I did with bold reluctance. Who do I see? What do I see? What would I like to say?

Unexpectedly, I made strong connection with my

younger self. I saw myself sitting on the bed at the right-hand side of my old bedroom. I was older than I expected, maybe nine, and wearing a yellow dress, white ankle socks, and red shoes. Clearly there was a combination of different time frames as the yellow dress I had when I was much younger. Her hair was grown out a little. What was my impression of her? What was she like? She seemed strong, assertive, cute like she was still growing. I put out my hand to take her out of there because I felt she didn't want to be left behind. I was sorry I left her alone.

But she immediately wanted to tell me that she was alright. That was a real relief to me because I had been so disconnected for so long, I thought I would encounter anger and resentment. It felt like she was intact and well. For that I was very grateful. In that moment, I was flooded with memories and images of trees, nature, dancing, running, and swimming. I had a real sense of fun, wildness, smiling, laughter, long grass, picnics, butterflies, the hill, freewheeling. Absolute freedom in the outdoors. It is a lasting image and one I hold dear.

Why would I tell you such a personal story?

As an adult it is sometimes hard to accept how long you have been ruled by the childhood context. I internalised a critical voice and believed it to be my own. Eventually, I doubted the existence of this wild part of myself. I felt empty inside. I always knew there must be more to me, for me, about me, but I couldn't hold onto the image for very long. The intuitive part was never fully quenched, and I felt its presence when I was unsettled or at odds with the world around me. But it never gave up trying to connect with me. It won't give up trying to connect with you. So, watch for the signs. Be open to the possibilities.

Now I have a clear connection to my younger self thanks to a powerful coaching experience with a coach who could handle both anger and painful loss without trying to fix or interpret it.
Now, nurture, nature, nutrition, and nostalgia help me to integrate this part of myself. It is from this place of wholeness and intuitive guidance that I coach other people to connect with that deeper part of themselves. Today I see it as an opportunity to share with others the ways in which you can encounter your essential self and live a happier joyous life with the kind of abundance that is never-ending, fulfilling, and available to all. There is always a story within the story looking for a safe space to be heard.

What is your true purpose in life? What things are you doing in your life that take you away from that? What steps can you take today that bring you closer? Begin each day with the intention of living out your true purpose in some small way.

The Divine Self

We are told, that we are created in the image and likeness of God and so we must have inherited divine existence. Why do we not readily access this? Are we overwhelmed, afraid, disbelievers? Too busy living in the real world. Too mad at God, the church, or are we too intelligent to fall for that? And yet, there is nothing more intelligent than the Divine self. Nothing more loving or powerful. Are we looking in all the wrong places for ourselves? We may think that something outside of ourselves will validate us, identify us, separate us from others.

You are not the car you drive, the address you hold, the promotion or award you just received, the clothes you wear, or the people you know. All these things only provide temporary feelings of wellbeing and happiness. You are not the mind that controls. You are not your body. Once all these things we identify with are removed, who are we? We are so much more. The divine self does not care for any of it, as it is 100% content as it is.

You came into the world as nothing less than a miracle. The sculptor of your own life and life experience. The divine self is part of something greater, with its connection to everything on earth, in the universe and beyond. It blissfully exists. Accessing and connecting to this part of yourself takes time and patience. There is nothing to put in and nothing to take out. Just sit at peace and be still.

You are this energy that circulates as you sit there. It is free, moves with grace, has no demands, and lights up as it goes. It lights up your body and mind but is not confined to it. It extends above and below you, around you and through you. It moves with such ease and extends out into the world. As it moves it is connected to everyone and everything and is nothing more than pure light and love. It moves eternally, bringing with it hope and understanding of death and grief. It brings us closer to those that we have lost and the realisation that we are never really separated. There is a beauty that cannot be equaled and a peace that is as rich as our wonder about it all. It is just so. Everything is a miracle.

A life of peace and ease.

A life of peace and ease is slow-moving and relaxed. There are the sounds of birds and lawnmowers busy in the distance. Creating that environment of peace and ease organically in the moment smells of Heaven and Beyond.

As the grass was cut for hay today, I pondered how everything must change, even nature. For progress, for harvest, to make way for new life nourishment. As I adjust to the loss of the long grass and hundreds of buttercups I walk in the now-open space and see clearly where I haven't changed and shifted for the changing season. Where I haven't nourished myself today and slipped back into old habits. I breathe into this knowing and feel the wisdom around me and vow not to become a forgotten field, overgrown, hidden, and never appreciated. The gate half-open looks like it is in no hurry to close and invites everyone to pass through. The breeze is very cleansing, and I find myself wanting to emulate Nature. To move with the seasons. To rain when the pressure gets too high, to shine when the sun is up, to move and sway, to die and be reborn with certainty.

The old stone sheds have stood the test of time and stand quietly with their lovely cool interior after a hard day's work done well. Right now, nothing needs to change the overgrown hedges, the cracks in the concrete, the missing slates on the roof. It is all at peace. I am at peace, and I am protective of this space and place. In this space there is no self judgement, success or failure, forgiveness, or resolution. There is no need because it is a perfect moment and I choose where the next moment comes from. Does it come from the past or the future? Does it sit with me here right now like the companion of the sun, moon, and stars? Right here, right now is peace and happiness. From this position of peace and happiness, I can make better choices to enjoy the life I was given. To find true purpose, to work to my full potential. To love fully. To experience Spiritual balance. I have it all. You have it all. You always did. That is my gift to you.

Recommended Resources

O'Donoghue, John. Anam Cara, Spiritual Wisdom from the Celtic World. Bantam Books 1999.

O'Donoghue, John. Benedictus, A blook of blessings. Bantam Press 2007.

Tolle, Eckhart. Stillness Speaks. New World Library, 2003. Tolle, Eckhart. The Power of Now. New World Library, 2005.

Tolle, Eckhart. Oneness with all life. Penguin Random House, 2018.

Chopra, Deepak. The 7 Spiritual Laws of Success. Amber-Allen, 2015.

Gawain, Shakti. Creative Visualisation. New World Library, 1995.

Ravikant, Kamal. Love Yourself Like Your Life Depends on It. HarperCollins, 2022

Ravikant, Kamal. Live Your Truth. Founderzen, 2013.

McKenna, Paul Change Your Life In 7 Days. Bantam Press, 2004.

McKenna, Paul. Positivity. Confidence, Resilience, Motivation. Welbeck, 2021.

Neff, Kristin. Self-Compassion. William Morrow, 2011.

Dean, Jeremy. Making Habits Breaking Habits. Oneworld, 2013.

Bungay Stanier, Michael. The Coaching Habit. Box of Crayons Press, 2016.

Brown, Brene. The Gifts of Imperfection. Hazelden, 2010.

Thubten, Gelong. A Monk's Guide to Happiness.

Yellow Kite, 2019. Oliver, Mary. Why I Wake

Early. Beacon Press 2005

Oliver, Mary. Thirst. Beacon Press, 2006 Kennedy, Mary and Ní Chinnéide, Deirdre. Journey to the well. Hachette Books, 2024.

Winfrey, Oprah. What I know for sure.

Bluebird, 2022. O'Morain, Padraig. Daily

calm. Yellowkite, 2020.

Pinkola Estes, Clarissa. Women Who Run with The Wolves. Ballantine Books, 1996

Acknowledgements

The idea for this book was born out of a small pink notebook covered in turquoise peacocks and vintage birdcages. I filled this notebook with meditations that I imagined and used for my own health and wellbeing. I am grateful that this planted the seed for something greater, this book called 'Being'.

Thank you to my editor, Anna Benn.
Gratitude to the staff from Creative Writing Ink.

I am truly grateful to my children who assisted me in any way they could. They were very resourceful, patient and kind, values that are very important to me.

www.ingramcontent.com/pod-product-compliance
Lightning Source LLC
Chambersburg PA
CBHW032044290426
44110CB00012B/943